好奇的
牛骚动

Mandarin

马西·沙夫

THE CURIOUS
COW COMMOTION

Mandarin

Marcy Schaaf

Dedication:

To Jessy and Jurnee,
the real-life stars of our story,

Your curiosity and sense of adventure have brought joy to our hearts and inspired the tale of "The Curious Cow Commotion." May your days be filled with laughter, love, and many more unforgettable adventures. Thank you for sharing your wonderful moment with us.

奉献精神：

致杰西和朱尼，
我们故事中现实生活中的明星，

你们的好奇心和冒险精神给我们带来了欢乐，并激发了"好奇牛骚动"的故事。愿您的日子充满欢笑、爱和更多难忘的冒险。感谢您与我们分享您的美好时刻。

Once upon a time,
in a cozy little town,
there lived a neighbor named
Mrs. Jenkins.
She had a secret that would
soon be found.

从前，在一个舒适的小镇上，住着一位名叫詹金斯夫人的邻居。

她有一个很快就会被发现的秘密。

Mrs. Jenkins, you see,
was quite a curious soul.
She loved to explore and
had quite the adventurous
goal.

你看，詹金斯夫人
是一个充满好奇心
的人。她喜欢探索
并且有相当冒险的
目标。

One sunny morning, she spotted a sight so rare. Cows in her neighbor's yard, grazing without a care!

一个阳光明媚的早晨，她发现了如此罕见的景象。邻居家院子里的牛，无忧无虑地吃草！

To warn her neighbors of this
curious delight,
Mrs. Jenkins picked up rocks,
with all her might.

为了警告邻居们这种奇怪的快乐，詹金斯夫人使出浑身解数捡起了石头。

She aimed for their window,
hoping they would see,
but with a loud crash,
she hit the sprinkler key.

她瞄准了他们的窗户，希望他们能看到，但随着一声巨响，她按下了洒水器的钥匙。

The water sprayed high,
a fountain of spray,
and in the midst of the chaos,
the cows began to sway.

水喷得高高的，像喷泉
一样，在一片混乱中，
牛群开始摇晃。

Splish, splash, they danced,
twirling around.
The cows turned the lawn into a wet,
muddy playground.

溅起，溅起，他们跳舞，旋转。
奶牛把草坪变成了潮湿、泥泞的游乐场。

Mrs. Jenkins panicked,
she needed help fast!
She waved her arms wildly,
hoping her neighbors would be
aghast.

詹金斯夫人惊慌失措，
她需要紧急帮助！
她疯狂地挥舞着手臂，
希望邻居们会感到震
惊。

Finally, they saw her and rushed
to the scene. Their faces turned
from shock to curious and keen.

最后，他们看到了她，并赶到了现场。他们的脸色从震惊变成了好奇和敏锐。

"Oh my goodness!" they said,
"Look at this display!"
The cows and the sprinkler turned
this into a special day.

"哦，我的天啊！"他们
说："看看这个展示！"奶
牛和洒水器让这一天变得特
别。

They all laughed and played in the
water's cool embrace.
Mrs. Jenkins had indeed gotten their
attention in this wild chase.

他们都在水清凉的怀抱中欢笑嬉戏。
詹金斯夫人在这场疯狂的追逐中确实引起了他们的注意。

Together, they herded the cows
back to their farm,
thanking Mrs. Jenkins for keeping
them from harm.

他们一起把奶牛赶回农场，感谢詹金斯夫人让它们免受伤害。

The cows waved their tails, saying goodbye with glee. Mrs. Jenkins was the hero of the day, as far as the eye could see.

牛们摇着尾巴，高兴地告别。就人们所见，詹金斯夫人是当天的英雄。

From that day forward,
Mrs. Jenkins was known,
as the lady who saved the
day, now with a cow of
her own.

从那天起，詹金斯
夫人被称为拯救世
界的女士，现在她
拥有了一头牛。

So remember, dear children,
when you see a cow in sight,
be curious like Mrs. Jenkins,
and everything will turn out
just right!

所以请记住，亲爱的孩子们，当你看到一头牛时，像詹金斯夫人一样好奇，一切都会好起来的！

The End!

The actual cow !!!

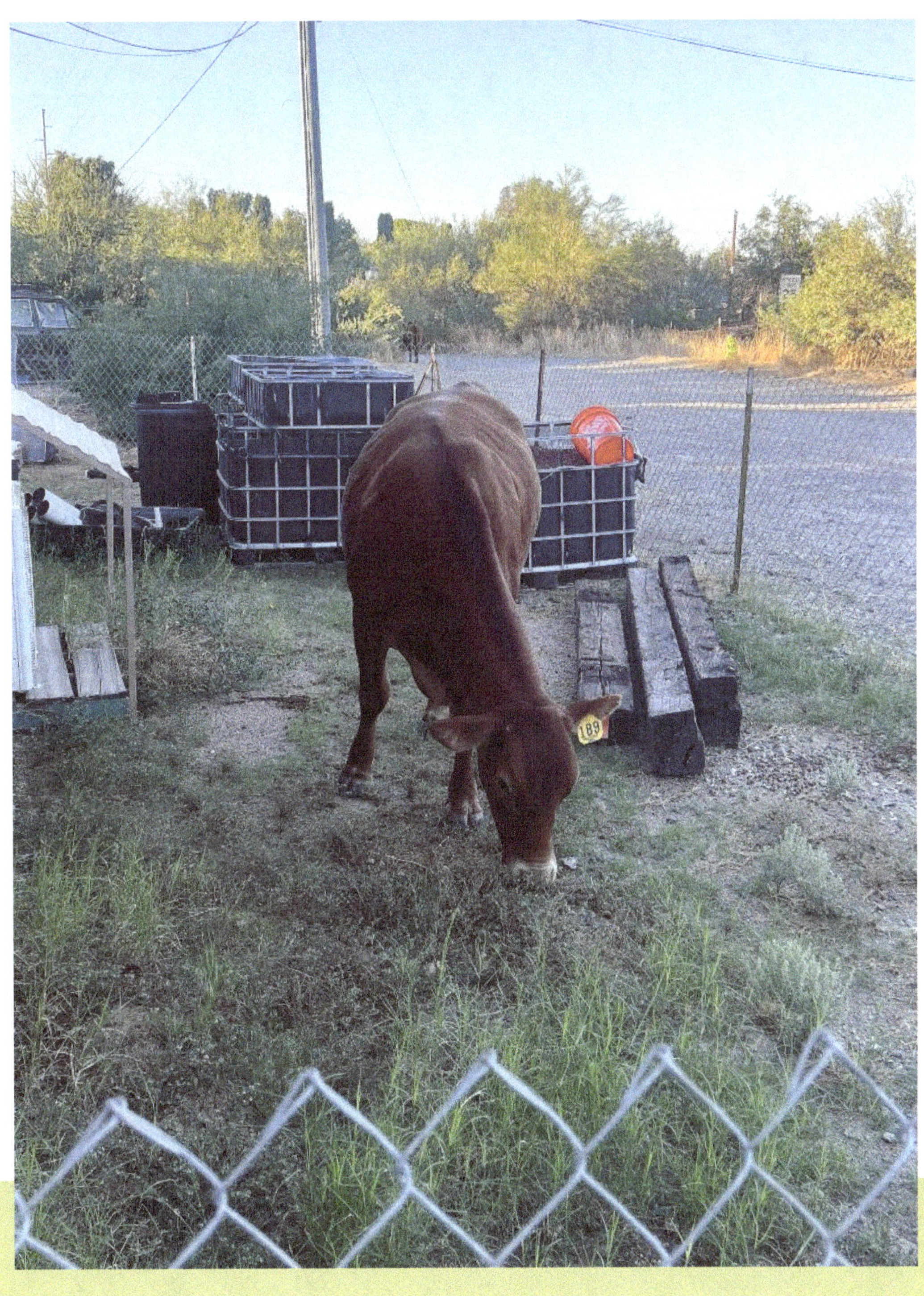

结束！

真正的牛！！！

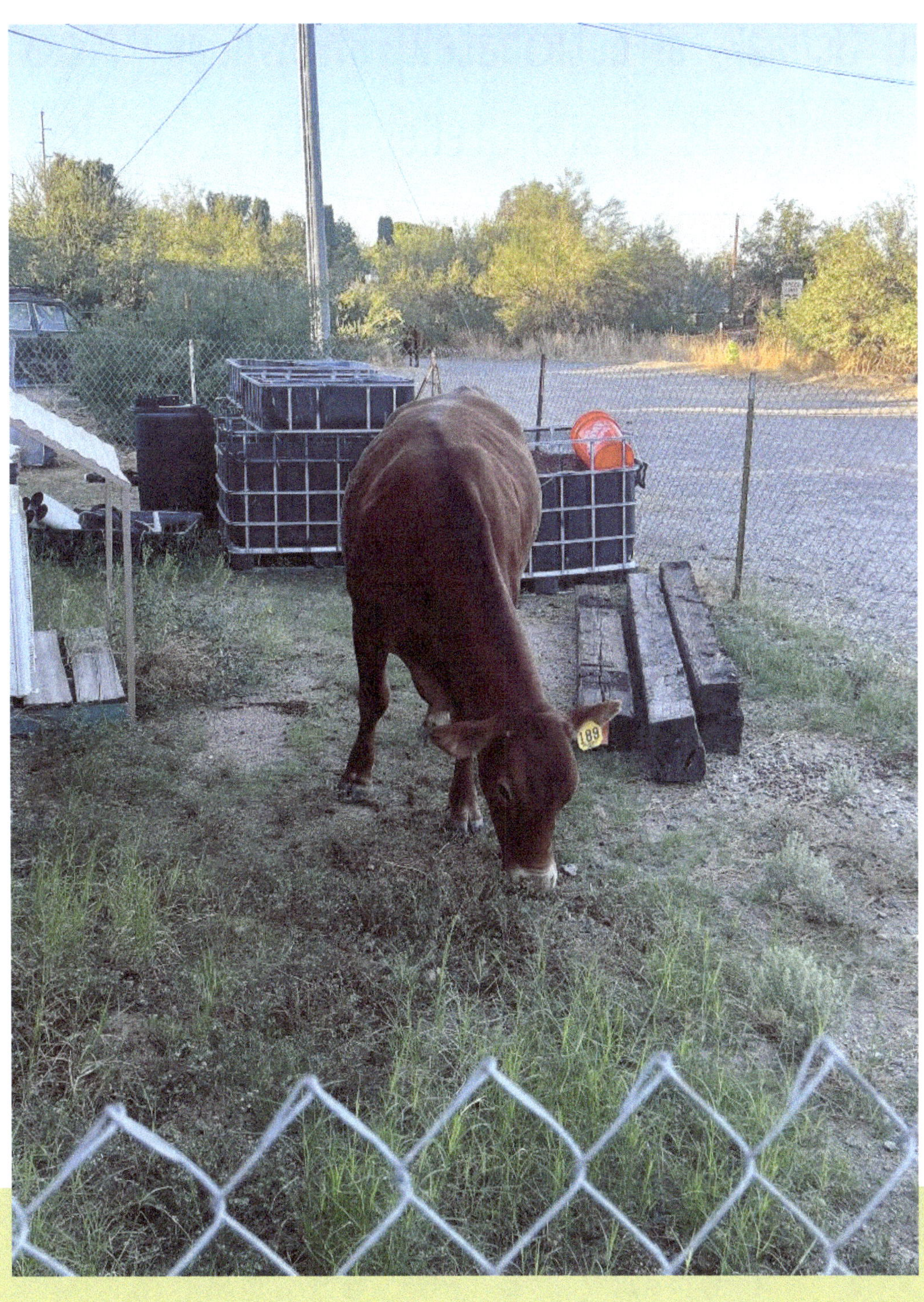

Author Bio:

Marcy Schaaf, affectionately known as "Moo" by her family, is a storyteller with a passion for weaving imaginative tales that enchant young hearts. Marcy finds joy in crafting stories that spark young minds' curiosity and ignite their sense of wonder. When she's not writing charming stories or being called "Moo" by her family, Marcy enjoys exploring and often spends her time traveling the world looking for her next tale. Her hope is that her stories will bring smiles, laughter, and a touch of magic to children all around the world.

作者简介：

马西·沙夫 (Marcy Schaaf) 被家人亲切地称为"Moo"，她是一位讲故事的人，热衷于编织充满想象力的故事来吸引年轻人的心。马西在编写激发年轻人好奇心并点燃他们的好奇心的故事中找到了乐趣。当玛西不写迷人的故事或不被家人称为"Moo"时，她喜欢探索，并经常花时间环游世界寻找她的下一个故事。她希望她的故事能为世界各地的孩子们带来微笑、欢笑和一丝魔力。